CliffsNotes™

1984

By Nikki Moustaki, M.A., M.F.A

IN THIS BOOK

- Learn about the Life and Background of the Author
- Preview an Introduction to the Novel
- Study a graphical Character Map
- Explore themes and literary devices in the Critical Commentaries
- Examine in-depth Character Analyses
- Reinforce what you learn with CliffsNotes Review
- Find additional information to further your study in CliffsNotes Resource Center and online at www.cliffsnotes.com

W9-AXJ-757

WILEY

Wiley Publishing, Inc.

About the Author:

Nikki Moustaki holds an M.A. in English and American Literature from New York University and an M.F.A in Creative Writing from Indiana University.

Publisher's Acknowledgments

Editorial

Project Editor: Tracy Barr
Acquisitions Editor: Greg Tubach
Editorial Administrator: Michelle Hacker
Glossary Editors: The editors and staff of Webster's New World Dictionaries

Composition

Indexer: York Production Services, Inc.
Proofreader: York Production Services, Inc.
Wiley Indianapolis Composition Services

CliffsNotes™ *1984*

Published by:
Wiley Publishing, Inc.
111 River Street
Hoboken, NJ 07030
www.wiley.com

Copyright © 2000 Wiley Publishing, Inc., Hoboken, NJ
ISBN: 978-0-7645-8585-2
Printed in the United States of America
15 14 13 12 11
1O/RU/RQ/QT/IN
Published by Wiley Publishing, Inc., Hoboken, NJ
Published simultaneously in Canada

Library of Congress Cataloging-in-Publication Data
Moustaki, Nicole.
    CliffsNotes 1984 / Nikki Moustaki.
        p. cm.
    ISBN 978-0-7645-8585-2 (alk. paper)
    1. Orwell,George, 1903–1959. Nineteen Eighty-Four--Examinations--Study guides. 2. Political fiction, English--Examinations--Study guides. 3. Science fiction, English--Examinations--Study guides. 4. Totalitarianism and literature. 5. Dystopias in literature. I. Title: 1984.

PR6029.R8 N642 2000
823'.912--dc21--dc21   00–037037
                                              CIP

For general information on our other products and services or to obtain technical support, please contact our Customer Care Department within the U.S. at 800-762-2974, outside the U.S. at 317-572-3993, or fax 317-572-4002.

Wiley also publishes its books in a variety of electronic formats. Some content that appears in print may not be available in electronic books.

Table of Contents

How to Use This Book

This CliffsNotes study guide on George Orwell's *1984* supplements the original literary work, giving you background information about the author, an introduction to the work, a graphical character map, critical commentaries, expanded glossaries, and a comprehensive index, all for you to use as an educational tool that will allow you to better understand *1984*. This study guide was written with the assumption that you have read *1984*. Reading a literary work doesn't mean that you immediately grasp the major themes and devices used by the author; this study guide will help supplement your reading to be sure you get all you can from George Orwell's *1984* CliffsNotes Review tests your comprehension of the original text and reinforces learning with questions and answers, practice projects, and more. For further information on George Orwell and *1984*, check out the CliffsNotes Resource Center.

CliffsNotes provides the following icons to highlight essential elements of particular interest:

Reveals the underlying themes in the work.

Helps you to more easily relate to or discover the depth of a character.

Uncovers elements such as setting, atmosphere, mystery, passion, violence, irony, symbolism, tragedy, foreshadowing, and satire.

Enables you to appreciate the nuances of words and phrases.

Don't Miss Our Web Site

Discover classic literature as well as modern-day treasures by visiting the CliffsNotes Web site at www.cliffsnotes.com. You can obtain a quick download of a CliffsNotes title, purchase a title in print form, browse our catalog, or view online samples.

LIFE AND BACKGROUND OF THE AUTHOR

The following abbreviated biography of George Orwell is provided so that you might become more familiar with his life and the historical times that possibly influenced his writing. Read this Life and Background of the Author section and recall it when reading Orwell's *1984*, thinking of any thematic relationship between Orwell's novel and his life.

Personal Background

George Orwell is the pen name of Arthur Blair, born in 1903 in Motihari, Bengal, India, during the time of the British colonial rule. Young Orwell was brought to England by his mother and educated in Henley and Sussex at schools.

Early Years

The Orwell family was not wealthy, and, in reading Orwell's personal essays about his childhood, readers can easily see that his formative years were less than satisfying. However, the young Orwell had a gift for writing, which he recognized at the age of just five or six. Orwell's first published work, the poem "Awake Young Men of England," was printed in the *Henley and South Oxfordshire Standard* when he was eleven years old.

Orwell attended Eton College. Because literature was not an accepted subject for boys at the time, Orwell studied the master |writers and began to develop his own writing style. At Eton, he came into contact with liberalist and socialist ideals, and it was here that his initial political views were formed.

Adult Years

Orwell moved to Burma in 1922, where he served as an Assistant Superintendent of Police for five years before he resigned because of his growing dislike for British Imperialism. In 1928, Orwell moved to Paris and began a series of low paying jobs. In 1929, he moved to London, again living in what he termed "fairly severe poverty." These experiences provided the material for his first novel, *Down and Out in Paris and London,* which he placed with a publisher in 1933.

About this time, while Orwell was teaching in a small private school in Middlesex, he came down with his first bout of pneumonia due to tuberculosis, a condition would plague him throughout his life and require hospitalization again in 1938, 1947, and 1950.

In 1933, Orwell gave up teaching and spent almost a year in Southwold writing his next book, *Burmese Days.* During this time, he worked part time in a bookshop, where he met his future wife, Eileen O'Shaughnessy. He and Eileen were he married in 1936, shortly before he moved to Spain to write newspaper articles about the Spanish Civil War.

In Spain, Orwell found what he had been searching for—a true socialist state. He joined the struggle against the Fascist party but had to flee when the group with which he was associated was falsely accused of secretly helping the Fascists.

By 1939, Orwell had returned to England. In 1941, he took a position with the British Broadcasting Corporation (BBC) as the person in charge of broadcasting to India and Southeast Asia. Orwell disliked this job immensely, being, as he was, in charge of disseminating propaganda to these British colonies—an act that went against both his nature and his political philosophy. In 1943, Orwell took a job more to his liking, as the literary editor of *The Tribune.*

Shortly after Orwell and Eileen adopted a son in 1944, Orwell became a war correspondent for the *Observer* in Paris and Cologne, Germany. Tragically, Eileen died in the beginning of that year, just before the publication of one of his most important novels, *Animal Farm.* Despite the loss of his wife and his own battle with poor health, Orwell continued his writing and completed the revision of *1984* in 1948. It was published early the next year with great success.

Orwell remarried in 1949 to Sonia Brownell, only a year before his own death of tuberculosis. He is buried in the churchyard of All Saints, Sutton Courtenay, Berkshire.

Literary Writing

Orwell's writing career spanned nearly seventeen years. Ironically, although Orwell didn't consider himself a novelist, he wrote two of the most important literary masterpieces of the 20th century: *Animal Farm* and *1984.* While these are the most famous novels of his career, his memoirs, other novels, and essential work as an essayist all contribute to the body of work that makes up important twentieth century literature.

In Orwell's writing, he sought truth. Even his fiction has elements of the world around him, of the wars and struggles that he witnessed, of the terrible nature of politics, and the terrible toll that totalitarianism takes on the human spirit. From the time he began to write at the age of twenty-four, Orwell longed to capture the struggles of "real" people, to live among the less fortunate, and to tell their stories. Of his own writing, Orwell has said that he writes because there is some kind of lie that he has to expose, some fact to which he wants to draw attention. Orwell certainly does this in *1984,* a novel fraught with political purpose, meaning, and warning.

INTRODUCTION TO THE NOVEL

The following Introduction section is provided solely as an educational tool and is not meant to replace the experience of your reading the novel. Read the Introduction and A Brief Synopsis to enhance your understanding of the novel and to prepare yourself for the critical thinking that should take place whenever you read any work of fiction or nonfiction. Keep the List of Characters and Character Map at hand so that as you read the original literary work, if you encounter a character about whom you're uncertain, you can refer to the List of Characters and Character Map to refresh your memory.

Introduction

Orwell's *1984*, like many works of literature, unmistakably carries with it literary traditions reaching back to the earliest of storytellers. Among the literary traditions that Orwell uses is the concept of *utopia*, which he distorts effectively for his own purposes. Utopia, or Nowhere Land, is an ideal place or society in which human beings realize a perfect existence, a place without suffering or human malady. Orwell did not originate this genre. In fact, the word *utopia* is taken from Sir Thomas More's *Utopia,* written in 1516. The word is now used to describe any place considered to be perfect.

In *1984,* Orwell creates a technologically advanced world in which fear is used as a tool for manipulating and controlling individuals who do not conform to the prevailing political orthodoxy. In his attempt to educate the reader about the consequences of certain political philosophies and the defects of human nature, Orwell manipulates and usurps the utopian tradition and creates a *dystopia,* a fictional setting in which life is extremely bad from deprivation, oppression, or terror. Orwell's dystopia is a place where humans have no control over their own lives, where nearly every positive feeling is squelched, and where people live in misery, fear, and repression.

The dystopian tradition in literature is a relatively modern one and is usually a criticism of the time in which the author lives. These novels are often political statements, as was Orwell's other dystopian novel, *Animal Farm*, published in 1945. By using a dystopian setting for *1984*, Orwell *suggests* the possibility of a utopia, and then makes very clear, with each horror that takes place, the price humankind pays for "perfect" societies.

Historical Background

Orwell wrote *1984* just after World War II ended, wanting it to serve as a warning to his readers. He wanted to be certain that the kind of future presented in the novel should never come to pass, even though the practices that contribute to the development of such a state were abundantly present in Orwell's time.

Orwell lived during a time in which tyranny was a reality in Spain, Germany, the Soviet Union, and other countries, where government kept an iron fist (or curtain) around its citizens, where there was little, if any freedom, and where hunger, forced labor, and mass execution were common.

Orwell espoused democratic socialism. In his essay, "Why I Write," published in 1947, two years before the publication of *1984*, Orwell stated that he writes, among other reasons, from the "[d]esire to push the world in a certain direction, to alter other peoples' idea of the kind of society that they should strive after." Orwell used his writing to express his powerful political feelings, and that fact is readily apparent in the society he creates in *1984*.

The society in *1984*, although fictional, mirrors the political weather of the societies that existed all around him. Orwell's Oceania is a terrifying society reminiscent of Hitler's Germany and Stalin's Soviet Union—complete repression of the human spirit, absolute governmental control of daily life, constant hunger, and the systematic "vaporization" of individuals who do not, or will not, comply with the government's values.

Orwell despised the politics of the leaders he saw rise to power in the countries around him, and he despised what the politicians did to the people of those countries. Big Brother is certainly a fusing of both Stalin and Hitler, both real and terrifying leaders, though both on opposite sides of the philosophical spectrum. By combining traits from both the Soviet Union's and Germany's totalitarian states, Orwell makes clear that he is staunchly against any form of governmental totalitarianism, either from the left or the right of the political spectrum.

By making Big Brother so easily recognizable (he is physically similar to both Hitler and Stalin, all three having heavy black mustaches and charismatic speaking styles), Orwell makes sure that the reader of *1984* does not mistake his intention—to show clearly how totalitarianism negatively affects the human spirit and how it is impossible to remain freethinking under such circumstances.

The Role of the Media

Orwell spent time in Spain during the time of Franco's Fascist military rebellion. Although he was initially pleased with what he considered to be the realization of socialism in Barcelona, he quickly saw that dream change; such a political climate could not maintain that kind of "ideal" political life. The group with which Orwell was associated was accused of being a pro-Fascist organization, a falsehood that was readily believed by many, including the left-wing press in England. As a reflection on this experience, in *1984*, Orwell creates a media service that is nothing more than a propaganda machine, mirroring what Orwell, as a writer, experienced during his time in Spain.

Orwell worked with the BBC during World War II when certain kinds of restrictions limiting what news could be disseminated were common, and he became disturbed by what he perceived to be the falseness of his work. It is noteworthy that Winston Smith, the main character in *1984*, works in the media and is responsible for creating what is, essentially, deceptive propaganda. In fact, it is Winston's position in the media that gives the reader the most insight into the duplicity of the society in which he lives and therefore, the society that Orwell most condemns.

The Setting

The setting of *1984* is Oceania, a giant country comprised of the Americas; the Atlantic Islands, including the British Isles; Australia; and the southern portion of Africa. Oceania's mainland is called Air Strip One, formerly England. The story itself takes place in London in the year 1984, a terrifying place and time where the human spirit and freedom are all but crushed. In the novel, war is constant. The main character, Winston Smith, born before the World War II, grew up knowing only hunger and political instability, and many of the things that he experiences are hyperboles of real activities in wartime Germany and the Soviet Union.

It is important to remember that Orwell based *1984* on the facts as he knew them; hunger, shortages, and repression actually happened as a result of the extreme governmental policies of these countries. The war hysteria, the destruction of the family unit, the persecution of "free thinkers" or those who were "different" or not easily assimilated into the party doctrine, the changing of history to suit the party's agenda, were all too real. Orwell's speculation of the future is actually a creative extension of how the masses were treated under Franco, Hitler, and Stalin.

By setting *1984* in London, Orwell is able to invoke the atmosphere of a real war-torn community, where people live in "wooden dwellings like chicken houses" in bombed-out clearings. His intent clearly was to capitalize on a memory that every reader, especially a British reader, was likely to have. London in *1984*, then, becomes not just a make-believe place where bad things happen to unknown people, but a very real geographical spot that still holds some connection for the modern reader.

In *1984*, the world is sliced into three political realms—the super states of Oceania, Eastasia, and Eurasia. Orwell drew these lines fairly consistent with the political distribution of the Cold War era beginning after World War II. Each of these three states is run by a totalitarian government that is constantly warring on multiple fronts. By creating an entire world at war, Orwell not only creates a terrifying place, but he also eliminates the possibility of escape for Winston, who is forced to live within his present circumstances, horrible and unremitting as they are.

Oceania's political structure is divided into three segments: the Inner Party, the ultimate ruling class, consisting of less than 2 percent of the population; the Outer Party, the educated workers, numbering around 18 to 19 percent of the population; and the Proles, or the proletariat, the working class. Although the Party (Inner and Outer) does not see these divisions as true "classes," it is clear that Orwell wants the reader to see the class distinctions. For a socialist such as Orwell, class distinctions mean the existence of conflict and class struggle. In Hitler's Germany and Stalin's Soviet Union, for example, the few people who comprised the ruling class had a much higher standard of living than the masses, but in these nations, as in *1984*, revolt was all but impossible.

A Brief Synopsis

Winston Smith is a member of the Outer Party. He works in the Records Department in the Ministry of Truth, rewriting and distorting history. To escape Big Brother's tyranny, at least inside his own mind, Winston begins a diary—an act punishable by death. Winston is determined to remain human under inhuman circumstances. Yet telescreens are placed everywhere—in his home, in his cubicle at work, in the cafeteria where he eats, even in the bathroom stalls. His every move is watched. No place is safe.

One day, while at the mandatory Two Minutes Hate, Winston catches the eye of an Inner Party Member, O'Brien, whom he believes to be an ally. He also catches the eye of a dark-haired girl from the Fiction Department, whom he believes is his enemy and wants him destroyed. A few days later, Julia, the dark-haired girl whom Winston believes to be against him, secretly hands him a note that reads, "I love you." Winston takes pains to meet her, and when they finally do, Julia draws up a complicated plan whereby they can be alone.

Alone in the countryside, Winston and Julia make love and begin their allegiance against the Party and Big Brother. Winston is able to secure a room above a shop where he and Julia can go for their romantic trysts. Winston and Julia fall in love, and, while they know that they will someday be caught, they believe that the love and loyalty they feel for each other can never be taken from them, even under the worst circumstances.

Eventually, Winston and Julia confess to O'Brien, whom they believe to be a member of the Brotherhood (an underground organization aimed at bringing down the Party), their hatred of the Party. O'Brien welcomes them into the Brotherhood with an array of questions and arranges for Winston to be given a copy of "the book," the underground's treasonous volume written by their leader, Emmanuel Goldstein, former ally of Big Brother turned enemy.

Winston gets the book at a war rally and takes it to the secure room where he reads it with Julia napping by his side. The two are disturbed by a noise behind a painting in the room and discover a telescreen. They are dragged away and separated. Winston finds himself deep inside the Ministry of Love, a kind of prison with no windows, where he sits for days alone. Finally, O'Brien comes. Initially Winston believes that O'Brien has also been caught, but he soon realizes that O'Brien is there to torture him and break his spirit. The Party had been aware of Winston's "crimes" all along; in fact, O'Brien has been watching Winston for the past seven years.

O'Brien spends the next few months torturing Winston in order to change his way of thinking—to employ the concept of *doublethink*, or the ability to simultaneously hold two opposing ideas in one's mind and believe in them both. Winston believes that the human mind must be free, and to remain free, one must be allowed to believe in an objective truth, such as $2 + 2 = 4$. O'Brien wants Winston to believe that $2 + 2 = 5$, but Winston is resistant.

Finally, O'Brien takes Winston to Room 101, the most dreaded room of all in the Ministry of Love, the place where prisoners meet their greatest fear. Winston's greatest fear is rats. O'Brien places over Winston's head a mask made of wire mesh and threatens to open the door to release rats on Winston's face. When Winston screams, "Do it to Julia!" he relinquishes his last vestige of humanity.

Winston is a changed man. He sits in the Chestnut Tree Café, watching the telescreens and agonizing over the results of daily battles on the front lines. He has seen Julia again. She, too, is changed, seeming older and less attractive. She admits that she also betrayed him. In the end, there is no doubt, Winston loves Big Brother.

List of Characters

Winston Smith Winston, the novel's protagonist, is staunchly against the Party. He finds unobtrusive methods to rebel, or at least he believes them to go unnoticed. He main desire is to remain human under inhuman circumstances.

Julia Winston's love-interest and ally. Julia also works in the Ministry of Truth. She is against the Party's doctrines, but she merely wants to break the rules, not change the society.

O'Brien Member of the Inner Party. A mysterious figure, O'Brien is at once Winston's enemy and his ally and is the reason for Winston's ultimate indoctrination to the Party. O'Brien is a personification of the Party, and much of the Party's doctrine is revealed through him.

Big Brother Leader of the Party. Big Brother is a god-like figure, all-present, all-powerful, and eternal—yet quite intangible.

Emmanuel Goldstein Leader of the Brotherhood. Orwell leaves ambiguous whether the Brotherhood actually exists or is merely propaganda perpetuated by the Party. Nevertheless, Goldstein, whether he exists or not, figures prominently as a foil to Big Brother.

Mr. Charrington Owner of the shop where Winston rents the room and a member of the Thought Police.

Parsons Winston's neighbor who ends up in the Ministry of Love with Winston, turned in by his own children.

Syme A Newspeak expert who works with Winston in the Ministry of Truth and is vaporized.

Ampleforth A poet-of-sorts who works with Winston in the Ministry of truth and also winds up in the Ministry of Love.

Character Map

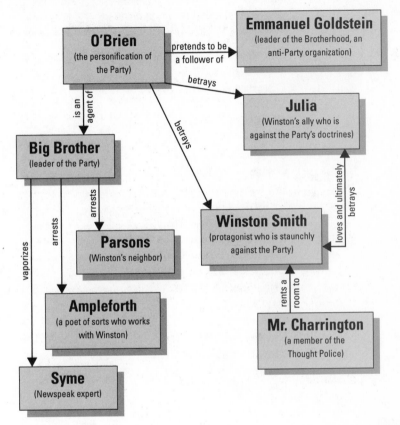

CRITICAL COMMENTARIES

The sections that follow provide great tools for supplementing your reading of *1984*. First, in order to enhance your understanding of and enjoyment from reading, we provide quick summaries in case you have difficulty when you read the original literary work. Each summary is followed by commentary: literary devices, character analyses, themes, and so on. Keep in mind that the interpretations here are solely those of the author of this study guide and are used to jumpstart your thinking about the work. No single interpretation of a complex work like *1984* is infallible or exhaustive, and you'll likely find that you interpret portions of the work differently from the author of this study guide. Read the original work and determine your own interpretations, referring to these Notes for supplemental meanings only.

Part One
Chapter I

Summary

On a bitter April day in London, Oceania, Winston Smith arrives at his small apartment on his lunch break. The face of Big Brother is everywhere. It is immediately obvious, through Winston's musings, that the political weather of Winston's London is grim and totalitarian. Winston pours himself a large drink and sets about to commit an act punishable by death—starting a diary. He believes he is fortunate because a small corner of his apartment is hidden from the telescreen—a device that allows him to be viewed and heard twenty-four hours a day by the authorities—or Big Brother. Here is where he begins the diary.

Winston is stuck by a pang of writer's block when he suddenly realizes that he doesn't know for whom he is writing the diary. In his panic, he begins to write a stream-of-consciousness account of a recent trip to the movies. While writing this, he has a memory of a significant happening earlier in the week, in which he was simultaneously attracted to and repelled by a young woman working in his building. He felt as though she was following him. He also remembers sharing a brief moment with O'Brien, a member of the Inner Party, an encounter in which Winston believes that O'Brien attempted to show solidarity with him against the tyranny of Big Brother. He continues writing, this time with more substantive material about his feelings on the current environment in which he lives. He is interrupted by a knock at the door.

Commentary

The opening image of the work sets the foreboding tone that prevails throughout as the reader is introduced to Winston Smith, the fatalistic protagonist of the novel, on a "cold day in April," when "the clocks were striking thirteen." Immediately, the author depicts a society in decay by describing a setting of "gritty dust," "hallways [smelling] of boiled cabbage and old rag mats," elevators (the lift) not working, and electrical current that is turned off during daylight hours.

The other main characters are introduced through Winston's perception of them. Julia, the dark-haired girl from the fiction department (who, in this part, is described but, as yet, unnamed), causes him "to feel a peculiar uneasiness which had fear mixed up in it as well as hostility, whenever she was anywhere near him." Winston suspects her to be a member of the Thought Police. Initially, he sees her as a symbol of social orthodoxy, that is, she possesses "a general clean-mindedness," an enthusiastic adherent to the Party line. Conversely, Winston feels a certain comradeship with O'Brien, predicated on his secretly held belief that "O'Brien's political orthodoxy was not perfect." Winston developed this impression when he and O'Brien had once exchanged glances. Big Brother (both a person and a concept) is introduced very early on in posters that appear in Winston's building bearing the caption "Big Brother Is Watching You." Finally, Emmanuel Goldstein, also, a person and a concept, is introduced during a hate session.

The political environment is detailed through Winston's musings, as well as narrative descriptions of specific political entities. At the heart of the political orthodoxy that exists is the process of controlling human thought through the manipulation of language and information. Crucial to manipulating the language and the information individuals receive are *doublethink* and *Newspeak*. Doublethink is the act of holding, simultaneously, two opposite, individually exclusive ideas or opinions and believing in both simultaneously and absolutely. Doublethink requires using logic against logic or suspending disbelief in the contradiction. The three slogans of the party—"War Is Peace; Freedom Is Slavery; Ignorance Is Strength"—are obvious examples of doublethink. The act of doublethink also occurs in more subtle details.

As Winston begins writing in the diary, he commits his first overt act of rebellion against the Party; he creates a piece of evidence that exists outside himself. He is still safe because no one else knows of his thoughts or his act, but the reader shares the ominous mood created when Winston observes, "Sooner or later they always got you." Winston, obviously, knows the significance of his act; nothing will ever be the same for him.

This first chapter introduces the reader to a host of significant issues and images that become motifs that set the mood for and recur throughout the novel. The reader is not so subtlety drawn into a world of constant duplicity, manipulation, and surveillance. The name of

Winston's apartment, "Victory Mansions," for example, creates a particular mental image for the reader that is immediately contradicted by Orwell's observation that the " . . . hallway smelt of boiled cabbage and old rags," the lift (elevator) seldom works, and the electricity is cut off during daylight hours—hardly a description one imagines of a structure with such an exalted name.

Big Brother, whose countenance purposely mirrors Stalin, and his pseudo omnipresence are introduced to the reader in the posters and on the telescreen. Although he never appears in person, Big Brother is the dictator of record in Oceania, and the posters carry the caption "Big Brother Is Watching You," enhancing the menacing feeling of an evil environment.

Orwell alerts the reader's senses of anticipation and dread in his depiction of the bureaucracy and political structure of Oceania: "The Ministry of Truth," which rewrites history to suit the occasion; "The Ministry of Peace," which functions to wage war; "The Ministry of Love," which maintains law and order and is "the really frightening one"; and the "Ministry of Plenty" coupled with the Thought Police, two minute hate sessions, and antithetical national slogans (War Is Peace, Freedom Is Slavery, and Ignorance Is Strength).

Glossary

(Here and in the following chapters, difficult words and phrases, as well as allusions and historical references, are explained.)

varicose ulcer an ulcer resulting from an abnormally and irregularly swollen or dilated vein ("varicose vein").

pig iron crude iron, as it comes from the blast furnace.

blue-bottle a bright, metallic-blue blowfly.

sanguine of the color of blood; ruddy: said especially of complexions.

Chapter II

Summary

The knock at the door is Winston's neighbor, Mrs. Parsons, who asks him to unclog her sink because her husband, Tom Parsons, who works with Winston in the Ministry of Truth, is not home. Winston obliges her and is accosted by her children, who call him a traitor, a thought criminal, and finally, Goldstein.

Winston returns home to continue the diary and again thinks of O'Brien. Winston recalls a dream seven years earlier in which a voice said to him, "We shall meet in the place where there is no darkness." He now believes this voice to be that of O'Brien's and is certain that, in some way or another, the prophecy of the dream will come to pass.

Back at the diary, Winston finally realizes who the audience is for his diary. He also realizes the inevitability of his death at the hands of the Thought Police.

Commentary

Winston's dream foreshadows what will take place later on in the book. The use of the phrase, "a place where there is no darkness," another recurring image in the novel, takes an ironic twist when this premonition of Winston's does not turn out as he expects. Winton attributes this phrase to O'Brien, a member of the Inner Party, who, later in the novel, meets Winston "in a place where there is no darkness"—the Ministry of Love, a prison.

The mutability of the past and the existence of fact through memory are prominent themes throughout *1984*. In this chapter, Winston begins to ask himself questions that will haunt him throughout the rest of the book; among them, how can an idea survive if the past is not allowed to exist? Both Hitler and Stalin distorted the past and rewrote history to maintain the illusion of supreme power. However, Orwell's intent is not merely to warn against the Hitlers (Fascists) and Stalins (Communists) of the world. Instead, his aim is to warn against the kinds of thinking and political processes that, although not as obvious as these two examples, ultimately make us receptive to more and more control.

In this chapter, Orwell further develops Winston's pessimistic, fatalistic character. He has been so convinced of and so assimilated by the Party's power and omniscience that he cannot imagine hiding any thought or action as he writes: "Thoughtcrime does not entail death: thoughtcrime IS death." Therefore, once he has committed his *thoughtcrime,* he is sure he will be discovered and punished (vaporized). Winston's goal essentially becomes not to stay alive, which he has no confidence he can accomplish, but to stay alive as long as possible.

Glossary

spanner [Chiefly British] wrench.

impedimenta things hindering progress, encumbrances.

Chapter III

Summary

This section begins with Winston dreaming of the deaths of his mother and sister. Although the past is unclear in his mind, he believes that he was somehow responsible. The dream scenery changes to a place that Winston calls the "Golden Country," and he imagines the dark-haired girl there. He awakes with the word "Shakespeare" on his lips.

Winston takes his place in front of the telescreen for the Physical Jerks, a daily exercise routine for Outer Party members. During the exercise, he thinks about the past and remembers a time as a child when he and his family ran into a bunker during a bombing. He is lost in the memory as he tries to touch his toes, causing the exercise director to shout at him from the telescreen.

Commentary

In this chapter, Orwell provides solid evidence to the reader that everything Winston thinks about his environment, as told to us through the narrator, is genuine. The telescreen is indeed watching him closely, and it is at this moment that the reader is fully aware of the reality of Winston's situation. His life and the political situation in Oceania are really as bad as they seem.

Literary
Device

An overview of Winston's perception of the past is given here in an attempt to assist the reader in understanding Winston's world and how it came to pass. The England-Britain-London of the past, Ingsoc in Oceania parlance (or, in Oldspeak, English Socialism) is briefly addressed. The premise of English Socialism is quite different from the society that prevails in Oceania. The Golden Country that Winston dreams about symbolizes the pastoral European landscape, the beauty obviously lacking in Winston's life. Winston waking with "Shakespeare" on his lips is part British nostalgia, part foreshadowing—Julia is named for Shakespeare's Juliet, reminding the reader of another story of forbidden love.

Orwell addresses, again, the problem of fact and memory. "The past . . . had not merely been altered, it had been actually destroyed. For how could you establish even the most obvious fact when there existed no record outside your own memory." Memory and history are major themes in the novel. Winston muses that the history books claim that the Party invented airplanes (a claim actually made by the German government during World War II). Yet Winston is certain that he remembers planes before the Party's existence. Of course, he has no way to prove it.

Glossary

dace any of various small, freshwater fishes related to the carp and minnow.

Chapter IV

Summary

In this chapter, Orwell gives a great deal of detail about Winston's job and the place in which he works, the Records Department in the Ministry of Truth, where his job is to rewrite history according to Party need. In this chapter, in addition to noting a few of his colleagues—among them Tillotson, a hostile co-worker in the next cubicle, and Ampleforth, a poet of sorts—Winston's task is re-write an article in which Big Brother commended a person who is now in the Party's disfavor. Winston creates a war hero, Captain Ogilvy, who has led an "ideal" life and was killed in battle. Winston writes a speech that Big Brother is supposed to have given, commending this hero that never existed. It strikes Winston that he could create a dead man but not a living one. Ogilvy, now in the records, exists on the same authority as genuine, living people.

Commentary

Style & Language

This chapter is full of details about Winston's work life: from the *speakwrite*, a contraption into which Winston speaks the articles that will be later written (*speaking* and *writing* here considered opposites), to the *memory holes* in which "records" are thrown, not to be remembered and documented, but to be destroyed. The reader should note that Orwell consistently names items, processes, and events antithetically to their intents, results, and purposes and thereby makes Winston's world more terrible and frightening. The function of the Ministry of Truth, for example, is to create lies; the function of the Ministry of Peace is to wage war.

Theme

Here the reader gets the full detail of Winston's work and a better view into the political system of his society. He is engaged in forging the past into something palatable to the Party's ideology: Big Brother is never wrong, heroes are those who put their own lives aside for the Party's benefit, and goods are always manufactured at a quantity beyond what is expected. Of course, none of it is true, and so follows

Winston's question, haunting him throughout the book: If a fact only exists in your memory, and yours alone, what proof is there that it really happened at all?

Glossary

pneumatic tube an inner tube, as in a pneumatic tire.

palimpsest a parchment, tablet, etc. that has been written upon or inscribed two or three times, the previous text or texts having been imperfectly erased and remaining, therefore, still partly visible.

Charlemange A.D. 742-814; king of the Franks (768-814): emperor of the Holy Roman Empire (800-814), also called Charles I or Charles the Great.

Julius Caesar 00?-44 B.C.; Roman general and statesman; dictator (49-44) of the Roman Empire.

Chapter V

Summary

At lunch, Winston's "friend," Syme lectures him on the principals of Newspeak, the only language that regularly *loses* words instead of gains them, effectively narrowing the range of thought. Syme says that, by the year 2050, everyone will be fluent in Newspeak. This idea disturbs Winston, but he dare not show it. Parsons, Winston's neighbor at Victory Mansions, joins them at the table and tells of his children who are constantly on watch for unorthodox behavior. Although seemingly uneasy about this, Parsons praises his children nonetheless. From the telescreen comes a loud announcement that, among other things, the chocolate ration is going up. Winston distinctly remembers that, just the day before, the ration was being reduced and he wonders if he is alone in this memory.

Winston sees the dark-haired girl from the Fiction Department (Julia) staring at him, and he is sure that she is a member of the Thought Police. He muses about many of the people he knows and whether they will eventually be vaporized or not.

Commentary

One of the major themes in 1984 involves language; when language is corrupted, thought is contaminated. Syme, who is the authority on Newspeak, gleefully informs Winston on its nuances. Whereas, for example, one would think that a language should grow in order to facilitate communication of invention, of newly discovered subtleties, and of changing times and attitudes, Syme explains that exactly the opposite is true. The language is streamlined by *destroying* words because some words, such as synonyms and antonyms, are not needed and only confuse issues. After all, the reasoning goes, "If you have a word like 'good,' what need is there for a word like 'bad'? 'Ungood' will do . . . better because it is an exact opposite . . . ." That said, "plusgood" need not be explained here; the same logic applies. Oldspeak contains "vagueness and useless shades of meaning." According to Syme, the mission of Newspeak, of course, is to narrow the range of thought to such a degree that *thoughtcrime* is impossible.

Newspeak, then, is a language created to control thought, thus controlling action. Orwell believed that the decline of language ultimately had political and economic consequences. He is warning that language can be a weapon. Newspeak was created only to control, not to enhance personal communication and expression. In the novel, this narrowing of thought facilitates *doublethink*, the primary instrument of control that the Party uses on its people.

Glossary

philologist someone who studies linguistics.

pannikin [Chiefly British] a small pan.

Chapters VI and VII

Summary

In Chapter VI, Winston confesses in his diary about a visit to an aging prostitute. This episode with the repulsive, objectionable prole prostitute exacerbates his desire for a pleasant sexual experience. Winston also thinks about his wife, Katharine, who has been out of his life for nearly eleven years. They separated because Winston could not stand Katharine's orthodoxy to the Party or her coldness toward him.

In Chapter VII, Winston writes of his hope that the proles, the working class, will rebel and change society. Due to their majority, Winston is sure that, if the proles would only become conscious of the fact that they could improve their situation, they could overturn the Party.

Winston also recalls a time in which he was sitting in a café next to three men who were later arrested and executed as enemies of the party. At one time, a photograph of these men had come across Winston's desk, proving that they were once in league with the Party and that, at the time of their supposed treason, they were at a Party function—proof that the men were forced to confess to false crimes. Winston threw the photograph into the memory hole for fear that this bit of real history and his effort to remember history as it actually happened would betray him as a thought-criminal.

Winston muses a bit on the Party's control over thought and realizes that he is writing the diary for O'Brien, the only person he believes to be on is side. He finishes this diary entry with the line "Freedom is the freedom to say that two plus two make four. If that is granted, all else follows."

Commentary

Literary Device

The Party controls even the most intimate of feelings and acts between human beings. Love and sex are conditioned out of people at an early age, and only loyalty to the party is intended to remain. Because Winston still has some memory of a time before the Party, he is "corrupt" in that he still has an active sex drive; he longs for the type of relationship no longer possible in his society. Winston's repressed sexuality, which causes him to respond and react in various ways and appears to be a significant force in his rebellion against the Party, is emerging as a motif in the novel.

Winston naively believes that the organization of the proles is the only way that society will be emancipated from the Party. Yet the proles have no leader and are more concerned with getting a cooking pot than improving their lives. The Party line runs "Proles and animals are free." Winston envies the proles' relative freedom and wishes they would suddenly become conscious of the Party's deceptions. Totalitarian regimes such as the one in Stalin's Soviet Union had similar demographics—the working class out-numbered the leaders by a huge margin—yet they failed to recognize or harness their potential and were, therefore, powerless to change anything.

Note that the themes of memory, history, and fact are again recalled—the photograph of the former Party members is the only piece of evidence that Winston has ever had that proves that the Party is deceptive, that Winston's memory is correct. Nevertheless, he destroys the photograph either from fear or from precedent. Of course, even had he kept the photograph, he could not have used it for any purpose other than to prove to himself that he was right.

The idea of right versus wrong, in terms of the events of history and common knowledge, is important in Chapter VII, as it is throughout the entire novel. Winston is sure that freedom is the freedom to think that what is right is right—that "two plus two makes four."

Glossary

subjection a being under the authority or control of another.

heresy any opinion (in philosophy, politics, etc.) opposed to official or established views or doctrines.

Chapter VIII

Summary

Winston decides to take a stroll through one of the prole neighborhoods. A bomb falls nearby, a common occurrence, but Winston is unhurt and continues walking, but not before he kicks a severed prole hand into the gutter. He enters a pub and begins speaking to an old man about the time before the war. The man refuses to answer Winston's questions with any kind of accuracy. Winston then returns to the little antique shop where he purchased the diary. He talks for a while with the shop's owner, Mr. Charrington, who sells him an antique paperweight and shows him an upstairs room. Winston is shocked that the room has no telescreen. Mr. Charrington also shows Winston a drawing of a church that he recognizes as a museum downtown and teaches him the beginning of a nursery rhyme.

Upon leaving the shop, Winston sees the dark-haired girl from the fiction department. He is sure that she is following him, and he imagines smashing her in the head with a cobblestone or the paperweight he has just purchased. He is paralyzed with fear. He also remembers again the dream in which O'Brien said to him, "We shall meet in the place where there is no darkness" and muses about when he will be detected as a thought-criminal. This chapter and Part I end with the repetition of Party's three slogans.

Commentary

The final chapter in Part I has Winston making a serious attempt to find a connection with the past. Winston knows that his actions mean certain torture and death, yet he continues to search, hoping that he is not alone, that someone else feels as he does. This is the first time in the novel that Winston actively reaches out to the past, to his curiosity and obsession with memory and history, and it is this action that seals his fate.

Mr. Charrington's antique shop, representing the past as it does, is a significant find. At the antique shop, Winston finds a paperweight and a fragment of a child's nursery rhyme, whose purposes are mysterious to him. These items become symbolic motifs in the novel. The paperweight, at this point in the novel, symbolizes the mystery and charm of the past, though later it will come to represent the relationship between Winston and Julia. The coral in the center of the paperweight represents rarity, and the fact that it is embedded in the glass and cannot be touched represent the problem in Winston's life. He wants to know the past, but too many obstacles surround it, preventing him access. The fragment of the nursery rhyme also becomes important later in the novel, functioning both as a thread tying together the main characters, as well as a representation of a kind of nostalgia that Winston is perpetually searching for.

Finally, Orwell closes the chapter with Winston thinking of the place where there is no darkness and the Party's terrifying slogans. By juxtaposing Winston's thoughts on "the place where there is no darkness" with the Party's slogans, Orwell reiterates the omnipotent and foreboding nature of the environment in which Winston lives and ominously foreshadows the link between O'Brien, the Party, and Big Brother.

Glossary

lackeys followers who carry out another's orders in the manner of servants.

bourgeoisie the social class between the aristocracy or very wealthy and the working class, or proletariat; middle class.

incongruous not corresponding to what is right, proper, or reasonable; unsuitable; inappropriate.

farthing a former small British coin, equal to one fourth of a penny.

Part Two
Chapter I

Summary

Winston is walking down a corridor at work when the girl from the fiction department, Julia, falls in front of him, hurting her arm. He notices that her arm is in a sling, and, although he is sure that she is a member of the Thought Police and therefore against him, he helps her to her feet. She slips a small folded scrap of paper into his hand and proceeds on her way. Winston must wait to open it, and when he finally does, it reads "I love you."

Winston has difficulty focusing for the rest of the day and tries to figure out a way to meet her. He sees her in the canteen a few times in the next few days but is unable to speak with her because of the lack of privacy. When he and she finally talk, they arrange to meet in Victory Square. At the meeting, Julia formulates a plan for the two of them to meet privately. They stand together, holding hands in the midst of a thick crowd watching a prisoner transport go by. Winston finds himself staring into the eyes of an aged prisoner instead of Julia's eyes as he would like, but he cannot risk looking directly at her.

Commentary

Part One was primarily about Winston, his motives, fears, desires, work life, and nature. This and the next couple of chapters develop Julia's character, which serves as a comparison and a contrast with Winston's character. Unlike Winston, Julia has no pre-Party history; consequently, she is a product of the developing political order. As a co-conspirator with Winston, Julia contrasts him in personality. Whereas Winston is pessimistically fatalistic, Julia is optimistically more matter of fact and accepts her lot for what it is. Julia is sensual, sexual, and practical. She and Winston will share the erotic affair that Winston has so ardently longed for.

In this chapter, Orwell introduces the true nature of Winston's conflict, which will inevitably lead to his doom. Until now, Winston has been merely another member of the Outer Party, going about his daily routine with little reason to attract attention to himself, except for the unorthodox thoughts inside his head and the diary that he begins in Chapter I. Winston now decides to act on his thoughts and feelings and to involve another person, a very risky venture considering the political environment in which he lives. Winston's rebellion against the Party now involves someone else and is no longer merely a *thoughtcrime*, but an overt action involving forbidden behavior with another individual. Clearly, the risk has heightened.

The suppression of language as communication between and among people, a common theme in the novel, recurs in this chapter with the explanation of how letters are either opened and read or are simply pre-written generic postcards on which the sender strikes out any sentences that do not apply. Also interesting is the fact that Orwell makes Julia a kind of writer. According to Orwell, true literature cannot exist in a totalitarian society because of the lack of freedom of spirit and freedom of expression. To be able to write, Orwell believed, a writer must be able to think fearlessly, and in thinking fearlessly, a writer could not be politically intimidated. Thinking fearlessly in Oceania is impossible.

The prisoners in the transport and the crowd's reaction to them are significant. The prisoners represent how the Party uses war to manipulate and control the masses. Winston identifies with the prisoners: Their faces are described as "sad" twice, and one prisoner in particular has "mournful" eyes and "nests of hair." Using the word "nest," a bird image, to characterize the prisoner's hair is ironic. Birds are generally seen as symbols for freedom and are used similarly in other places in the novel as well. Winston stares into the prisoner's eyes while thinking of Julia. This moment foreshadows Winston and Julia's arrest later in the novel.

Glossary

niggling stingy.

Mongolian of Mongolia, its peoples, or their languages or cultures.

Chapters II and III

Summary

Winston and Julia meet in the countryside. They talk a bit in the hideout that Julia has frequented with other men. They walk to the edge of a pasture, which Winston remembers from his dreams as the Golden Country. A bird lands on a branch near the couple, and Winston muses on its presence. Returning to the hideout, Winston and Julia make love. Winston discovers that Julia likes physical intimacy, unlike his former wife, and partakes in it quite frequently with Party members. Winston is happy in the knowledge that corruption and unorthodox acts happen often within the Party. They leave the hideout and agree to meet there again; instead, they meet in the belfry of a ruined church.

Julia tells Winston more about herself in the belfry, especially about her job, her love affairs, and her hatred of the Party. Winston and Julia discuss being caught. "We are the dead," Winston says to her. Julia is not convinced and keeps a more positive attitude. She draws a map in the dust of the place where they will meet again.

Commentary

Character Insight

Julia personifies the psyche of the oppressed individual under absolute despotic rule who suppresses individuality, creativity, and personal human relationships. She seems to be an absolute orthodox member of the Party, but in her "personal" time represents the exact opposite of what a Party member should be: She is at once in the Junior Anti-Sex league and participates in sexual activity with Party members. She prepares banners for Hate Week, while believing that those kind of Party functions are wholly without value. Everyone in Winston's immediate world demonstrates a kind of apparent social-political schizophrenia, believing one way and behaving another.

Literary
Device

The Golden Country where Winston and Julia meet alone for the first time is the symbolic motif that developed when Winston dreamt earlier in the novel about Julia being there and flinging off her clothes. The bird in the pasture is clearly a symbol for freedom—the kind of freedom that Winston desires. "For whom, for what, was that bird singing?" Winston asks himself. "No mate, no rival was watching it. What made it sit at the edge of a lonely wood and pour its music into nothingness?" These are questions Winston should be asking himself of his new relationship with Julia and, in fact, of his relationship with Big Brother. The bird is everything Winston is not but wishes to be.

The memory of the incident with Winston's wife, Katharine, is significant in that it describes a more orthodox or acceptable sexuality in Katharine, and it introduces another symbol: the two different colored flowers growing from the same root. The two flowers are Winston and Katharine or Winston and Julia, and the root symbolizes what the two have in common that sustains their natural individuality and different*ness*. Both are from the same root but are quite different in their philosophies.

The conversation at the end of Chapter III illustrates the fundamental differences between Winston and Julia: Winston is the eternal pessimist and Julia the eternal optimist. When Winston says, "We are the dead," Julia responds, "We are not dead yet." Julia brushes his statement aside and, in her usual manner, focuses on the physical by embracing him. Julia is preoccupied with physicality, while Winston is more introspective. Being against the Party, however, is enough to keep them connected.

Glossary

bluebells any of various plants with blue, bell-shaped flowers, such as the harebell, Virginia bluebell, etc.

etiolated pale and unhealthy.

knoll a hillock; mound.

incredulity unwillingness or inability to believe; doubt; skepticism.

thrush any of a large family of passerine birds, including the European song thrush and blackbird.

belfry a bell tower.

Chapter IV

Summary

Winston strikes a deal with Mr. Charrington, owner of the junk shop where Winston bought the diary and the glass paperweight, to rent the upstairs room for his affair with Julia. Waiting for Julia, Winston recognizes a song that a prole woman below his window is singing—a popular song written by a *versificator*—a machine that writes songs with no human intervention. He muses on the folly of taking the room and what it will eventually mean—capture and death.

Julia arrives, bringing Inner Party luxuries: real coffee, sugar, bread, jam, and tea. Julia paints her face with make-up and puts on perfume, all illegal items. Winston and Julia make love and fall asleep. After waking, Julia notices a rat poking its head through a hole near the baseboard. Winston reveals that he's afraid of rats, and Julia comforts him, promising to fix the hole. Winston begins the nursery rhyme that Mr. Charrington taught him a few weeks back, and Julia mysteriously finishes most of the verse—something her grandfather taught her. Winston looks at the glass paperweight and muses about it and what it symbolizes for himself, Julia, and their life together.

Commentary

The lyrics that the prole woman sings mirror the feelings that exist in Winston about his relationship with Julia, even if he does not know it as he hears them. He is becoming much more fond of Julia, to the point of becoming upset when she must break plans with him. In fact, Winston and Julia are beginning to live like "real" people now, like people of the past who luxuriated in the kinds of freedoms forbidden in their current situation. This chapter sets up a certain domesticity between them, a kind of comfort previously unavailable to them. But that comfort is deceptive, and Winston is aware of that fact, even if Julia is not. He is sure that they will be caught; the only question in Winston's mind is when.

Whenever a detail recurs or is emphasized, the reader should be certain to pay attention to its meaning or function. This chapter emphasizes, introduces, or returns to symbols mentioned previously: Winston's fear of rats, his nightmare, the nursery rhyme, and the paperweight. The rat poking his head through the wall foreshadows two separate events, both having to do with the couple's eventual capture. Winston is terrified of rats, a fact that is his breaking point later in the novel. The picture of St. Clement's Dane, aside from sparking another round of nursery rhymes, becomes the couple's downfall.

While Julia comforts Winston about the rat, he muses about a recurring nightmare in which he is in front of a wall of darkness and, although he knows what horrible thing is behind the wall, he does not have the courage to face it before waking. What is behind the wall is both symbolic and real: Behind the metaphoric wall is Winston's fate; behind the real wall in the room where he and Julia meet is the telescreen that reveals them.

Winston describes Julia knowing a piece of the nursery rhyme as a *countersign*, a secret signal that is still a mystery to him. He does know, however, that the rhyme ends with "*a chopper to chop off your head!*"— foreshadowing that does not bode well for Winston. Why everyone seems to know this rhyme except himself boggles Winston. Not knowing the rhyme sets him apart from others yet again—he is the perpetual outsider.

Finally, the image of the paperweight returns, this time as a symbol for the relationship between Winston and Julia. Winston sees it as a symbol of himself, feeling that he is actually inside the paperweight with Julia and that they are the coral "fixed in a sort of eternity at the heart of the crystal." Because most of Winston's perceptions are ironic, the reader must by this time be aware that a statement as boldly optimistic as this one will eventually crumble in the end. There is no such thing as "eternity" in Oceania, except where Big Brother is concerned.

Glossary

countersign a secret word or signal which must be given to a guard or sentry by someone wishing to pass; password.

Chapters V and VI

Summary

Winston is back at work, and Syme, the Newspeak expert, has vanished. Preparations for Hate Week are going on all over London.

Winston and Julia still meet in Mr. Charrington's room over the junk shop. Both are now aware that what they have together cannot last long. They talk of the war, which Julia believes is not truly happening, and they talk of people being vaporized. They daydream about being married and about engaging in active rebellion against the Party. Winston tries to make Julia understand that history is constantly being altered, but Julia does not see the significance in that fact. She is not interested in the past or the next generation of people; she is only interested in her relationship with Winston.

Back at work, O'Brien, an Inner Party member, approaches Winston and compliments him on his articles in the *Times*. O'Brien speaks to Winston about Syme, who is now an *unperson* and not to be discussed. Winston takes this conversation as a sign that O'Brien is on his side. O'Brien offers to lend Winston a copy of the latest edition of the Newspeak dictionary and gives Winston his address. Winston believes that this is the moment he has been waiting for, but he also realizes that by taking this step, he is destined for an early grave.

Commentary

Chapter V serves as a transition in time and as a way to fill the reader in on the details of the months that Orwell has skipped. This chapter also highlights the differences between Winston and Julia. Even though Winston now has an ally in Julia, he is still essentially alone in his thinking.

This chapter also serves to introduce the fact that Syme has been vaporized, enabling O'Brien to reference him in the next chapter and thus key Winston in to O'Brien's possible unorthodoxy. Syme's disappearance also serves as the basis of the relationship between Winston and O'Brien. Note that Winston predicted Syme's disappearance earlier in the novel; furthermore, this meeting between Winston and O'Brien had been foreshadowed in Chapter I, when Winston relates the eye contact made between him and O'Brien.

Winston interprets O'Brien's offer of the dictionary as an obvious ruse; he truly believes that his assumption about O'Brien's faithlessness to the Party is correct. Winston realizes at this moment that that he will follow through with O'Brien's summons. This decision is the turning point, or climax, in the story. All the events thus far in the novel have led to this moment. When Winston makes this irrevocable decision, he is at his greatest personal development. Although he could choose to turn away from destiny, he chooses instead to embrace it. From this point forward, fate takes over, and Winston is powerless to stop what comes to pass.

Glossary

bunting   a thin cloth used in making flags, streamers, etc.

Chapters VII and VIII

Summary

Awakening from a troubling dream, Winston tells Julia that he is responsible for the death of his mother. He recalls being hungry as a child and begging for food. One day, he stole a piece of chocolate from his small, weak sister and ran outside to eat it, not returning for a few hours. That was the last time he saw his mother and sister. The memory of Winston's mother holding his sister provokes him to think about the proles and the fact that they remain human, despite the society in which they live.

Winston and Julia discuss their relationship and how they will feel when they inevitably get caught. Julia is certain that, although both of them will confess, the Party is unable to make them believe their confessions, that it cannot "get inside you." Winston agrees.

Winston and Julia go to O'Brien's house, where they confess to O'Brien that they are enemies of the Party. O'Brien explains the secret Brotherhood, a loosely formed group committed to eliminate the Party, and initiates Julia and Winston into the group. The two swear to many perform many acts but refuse to never see each other again. O'Brien makes arrangements for Winston to receive a copy of "the book," Goldstein's heretical work. O'Brien says to Winston, "We shall meet again—" and Winston finishes the sentence, "In the place where there is no darkness?" O'Brien answers in the affirmative. Before Winston leaves, he asks O'Brien if he knows the last lines to the nursery rhyme that Mr. Charrington began for him earlier in the story, and O'Brien finishes it, much to Winston's surprise.

Commentary

Winston's memory of his mother and his sister serves to give the reader more insight into Winston's past and thus more insight into his character as an adult, into his motivations and why he does the things he does. He remembers a time when a gesture, such as embracing a child, could be done merely for the sake of itself, without catering to a political purpose. This memory reminds him of the proles, who do things just to do them, unlike Party members, who do things only because of their duty to Big Brother. Winston feels that the proles are the only hope for society to regain its humanity.

Winston's thoughts about the proles lead to one of the most important conversations between Winston and Julia. They discuss what they will do when caught. Although they know that they will confess to every detail, they are both sure that their actual *feelings* cannot be altered, that Big Brother can never get to the inner workings of the heart. They agree that the Party will make them inform on each other, but it will not be able to make them stop loving each other. This conversation is one of the greatest ironies in the novel and foreshadows what ultimately occurs between Winston and O'Brien and Winston and Julia.

Winston makes good on his decision to speak to O'Brien, in hopes that O'Brien has a solution to Big Bother's tyranny. When Winston learns that a secret Brotherhood really does exist, he and Julia are eager to join, even though O'Brien tells them the horrific consequences. Winston and Julia feel so strongly in their hatred of Big Brother and the Party that they are willing to do anything to help the Brotherhood, with one exception: they refuse to never see each other again.

The couple's honesty with O'Brien ultimately leads to their destruction as a couple, an irony that comes back to them at the end of the novel. O'Brien tells the couple that, if they survive, they may become unrecognizable to each other, that they may become entirely different people. Here Orwell foreshadows later events. The fact that O'Brien knows the ending to the nursery rhyme is noteworthy in that it signifies the beginning of the end for Winston. The fact that the ending comes from O'Brien is chilling considering the events that take place later in the story, when O'Brien effectively "ends" Winston as the reader knows him.

Glossary

superfluous being more than is needed, useful, or wanted; surplus; excessive.

simian of or like an ape or monkey.

stoneware a dense, opaque, glazed or unglazed pottery containing clay, silica, and feldspar and fired at a high heat.

sordid meanly selfish.

beseech to ask (someone) earnestly; entreat; implore.

clamorous loudly demanding or complaining.

remonstrances protests, complaints, or expostulations.

catechism a formal series of questions and answers.

Chapters IX and X

Summary

Winston is exhausted after working many long hours in the Ministry of Truth, helping to "rectify" the misinformation in all of the documents published by the Party for the past five years. As a result of a change in enemy, history must be rewritten. Having received "the book" from an anonymous person from the Brotherhood at a Hate Week rally earlier, Winston takes it to the room over Mr. Charrington's shop and begins to read, first alone and then to Julia. The book contains the history and ideology of the Party. Winston muses on what he has read in the book and realizes that it did not tell him anything new; Winston already knew the *how* of the Party's doctrine, but what he really wants to know is the *why*.

Winston falls asleep with Julia. When they wake, they discuss the prole woman outside hanging the laundry and singing and remember the singing bird they saw on the day they first met. Suddenly, a voice from behind the picture on the wall says, "You are the dead." Behind the picture is a telescreen. Winston and Julia are captured, and Mr. Charrington turns out to be a member of the Thought Police.

Commentary

Chapters IX and X signify the culmination of all of the novel's previous events; Winston believes he is now a part of the secret Brotherhood and revels in his new status, feeling comfortable for the first time in the novel. He begins to let down his guard and feel that he is beyond capture. The book O'Brien gives him provides Winston with the hope that the society of Oceania can eventually change. Like Winston, the reader is lulled into false security, thinking that the future is looking brighter. From all previous events, however, and with the predominance of irony throughout the story, one should realize that the opposite of what is on the surface in this story is generally the case.

The two sections that Winston reads from in the book—*The Theory and Practice of Oligarchical Collectivism*—take up most of the action in Chapter IX. This rambling political treatise incorporates several views, including those of Karl Marx and Leon Trotsky, on economic theory, class struggle, and other socio-political issues. This section also gives the reader more insight into the history and ideology of Oceania. By including this excerpt, Orwell stalls the action of the story in order to emphasize its anti-totalitarianism stance. In addition, the book shows that the entire world is basically the same as Oceania, although the two other countries call their brands of totalitarianism by different names. In this way, Orwell effectively makes escape for Winston and Julia impossible.

These chapters are full of the symbolism and recurring images and themes that persist throughout the novel. The prole woman who Winston once saw as dumb and ignorant now comes back as "beautiful" and is a symbol for the freedom that he and Julia will never have. The prole woman's singing recalls the bird that the couple saw that first day they met, the symbol of ultimate freedom and action for action's sake. Winston remarks that the bird was singing for them on that day, but Julia realizes that the bird was singing just to sing, nothing more.

When the couple is caught, Mr. Charrington's voice comes through the telescreen and repeats what the couple says, just as he has done earlier in the story when he pretended to be a harmless old man. Mr. Charrington finishes the nursery rhyme with its chilling and foreshadowing conclusion, giving closure to that bit of symbolism—the rhyme is complete, as is the end of the affair between Winston and Julia. The telescreen was hidden behind the drawing of the church, a symbol of sanctity and sanctuary; even the church is profane, having been the vehicle for surveillance and capture.

The glass paperweight returns as a symbol and is smashed during the couple's capture. Winston remarks that the coral that was formerly inside the paperweight is actually much smaller outside the glass. The paperweight represents Winston and Julia's relationship; their relationship, like the coral, is revealed and is bare and small beneath the eyes of Big Brother.

Neither Winston nor Julia makes any attempt to avoid capture; they submit without fighting. They are pure products of the society in which they live, finding it inconceivable to openly struggle against the forces of Big Brother. In the end of Part Two, the two are separated and are surely aware of their doom.

Glossary

gelatinous like gelatin or jelly; having the consistency of gelatin or jelly.

haranguing delivering a long, blustering scolding.

Oligarchical having to do with a form of government in which the ruling power belongs to a few persons.

Neolithic Age designating or of an Old World cultural period (*c.* 8000–3500 B.C.) characterized by polished stone tools, pottery, weaving, stock rearing, and agriculture.

meritorious having merit; deserving reward, praise, etc.

empirical relying or based on practical experience without reference to scientific principles.

ruminant of the cud-chewing animals.

Socialism any of various theories or systems of the ownership and operation of the means of production and distribution by society or the community rather than by private individuals, with all members of society or the community sharing in the work and the products.

cyclical of, or having the nature of, a cycle.

cardinal of main importance; principal.

titular existing only in title; in name only.

lingua franca any hybrid language used for communication between different peoples.

stratified classified or separated into groups.

ossified settled or rigidly fixed in a practice, custom, attitude, etc.

vilifies uses abusive or slanderous language about or of.

truncheons [Chiefly British] sticks or billy clubs, as used by the police.

Part Three
Chapter I

Summary

Winston finds himself inside the Ministry of Love in a cell with no windows and a telescreen watching his every move. He meets a drunk woman, a cell mate, who tells him that her name is also Smith and that she could be his mother, a fact that Winston cannot deny. Winston thinks of Julia and O'Brien. Ampleforth, the poet, Winston's coworker, is put into the cell with Winston. They discuss their "crimes," and Ampleforth is called out of the cell to Room 101. Parsons, Winston's orthodox neighbor is put into the cell, much to Winston's surprise.

Winston begins to think about Julia and what is happening to her. He believes that she is suffering, perhaps more than he is, and he decides that he would take double the pain she receives if doing so would spare her, but he realizes that this is just an intellectual decision. After a few ugly incidences involving the other prisoners in the cell, O'Brien comes in to get Winston. Winston initially believes that O'Brien is also caught but soon realizes that O'Brien has betrayed him.

Commentary

The events of this chapter are the realization of the inevitable— Winston is caught, just as he knew he would be the moment he began the diary. Winston also predicted that he would be held in the Ministry of Love, but did not expect that he would be there with people he supposed to be beyond reproach: Ampleforth, previously described as an ineffectual, dreamy creature, and Parsons, the highly enthusiastic Party-supporter who seemed to embody every quality the Party looked for in an Outer Party member.

Theme

Ampleforth believes he has been captured because he allowed the word "God" to remain at the end of a line of poetry because he needed the rhyme. Orwell broaches the theme of oppression of writers here again; Orwell, in his essay "The Prevention of Literature" (1946), asks the question, "Even under the tightest dictatorship, cannot the individual writer remain free inside his own mind and distill or disguise his unorthodox ideas in such a way that the authorities will be too stupid to recognize them?" Clearly, Orwell puts this question to the test, and Ampleforth suffers for it: The writer cannot remain free under totalitarianism.

Literary Device

Winston's statement about taking Julia's pain for himself is noteworthy here and soon comes back to haunt him. It foreshadows the critical event that eventually takes place between Winston and O'Brien and, ultimately, Winston's allegiance to his own feelings. Even as he says he will take Julia's pain, Winston knows that saying a thing and actually doing it are quite different, a realization that features in what eventually comes to pass between Winston and O'Brien. Winston *knows* that he loves Julia but does not, at this moment, *feel* love for her. The beginning of the end is near, and the fact that Winston's love for Julia is transforming into an intellectual exercise rather than a feeling of the heart foreshadows the change that occurs within Winston once O'Brien is through with him.

Winston knows now that the Ministry of Love is the "place where there is no darkness"; indeed, the lights never turn out. Here is another example of previous foreshadowing and irony: Winston certainly took his premonition to mean something much the opposite.

Chapters II and III

Summary

Winston is lying on a camp bed, where he has been for many days, being tortured almost constantly. O'Brien oversees Winston's "treatment." Finally, O'Brien personally takes over, torturing Winston when he does not give the correct answer to the questions O'Brien asks, many of which have to do with memory and objective truth.

O'Brien finally answers Winston's primary question, the question that has haunted him throughout the story: the *why* of the Party's behavior. Winston also learns that he is thought to be insane, and O'Brien, who acts strangely like Winston's friend, says that he will cure him. O'Brien allows Winston to ask him whatever he wants, and O'Brien seems to answer honestly.

In Chapter III, Winston enters the second stage of his "reintegration," *understanding*. Here, in his conversations with O'Brien, Winston learns about the Party's ideology and debates with O'Brien about the spirit of Man. Winston is able to look at himself in the mirror, a ruined, crushed human being, for which O'Brien mocks him. Winston discovers that Julia has betrayed him, but he has not yet betrayed Julia. Finally, O'Brien tells Winston what he knew all along—that he will eventually be shot—but is ambiguous about when.

Commentary

Winston's horrors and fear are brought to light in these chapters: He is betrayed by Julia and O'Brien, he is tortured and ruined, and every hope he had for a future without the Party is destroyed. Winston learns that Goldstein's book was written partially by O'Brien and that Big Brother exists just as the Party exists, eternal and omnipotent.

These chapters function much like the chapters of "the book," which Winston read earlier in the story; both serve to answer unanswered questions about the Party and its ideology. However, these chapters are more revealing and shed light on many of the things Winston has wondered about throughout the novel. He always understood *how* the Party wielded its power, but he never understood *why*; O'Brien explains to him that the Party seeks power solely for the sake of power, ironically like the bird or the prole woman singing just to sing, as Julia had observed earlier.

O'Brien tries to make Winston understand and employ the concept of *doublethink*; doing so will be Winston's only salvation, but Winston finds mustering the mental strength to do so difficult. This unwillingness to use *doublethink* has been Winston's downfall from the beginning and ultimately proves to be his breaking point.

Again the theme of the importance of objective truth returns. Here, Winston takes the position that memory and objective truth must win out over falsehood because the Party cannot destroy memory. O'Brien is set on proving Winston wrong in this case. O'Brien tells Winston that the Party is far superior to Nazi Germany or the Russian Communists because, unlike those other regimes whose enemies were eventually turned into martyrs, the Party refuses to let a stray thought get through. *Controlling all thought* is the Party's power, a power that will remain timeless.

Here Orwell takes totalitarianism a step further—into the mind. The equation that Winston writes in his diary, $2 + 2 = 4$, comes back to haunt him; it is the one objective truth that Winston cannot give up. The equation is the sticking-point between Winston and O'Brien and ultimately becomes the proof of Winston's reintegration. If Winston can believe that $2 + 2 = 5$, then the Party has gotten inside of him.

O'Brien knows about every "criminal" activity that Winston has engaged in to this point—even something as "minor" as Winston's memory of the photograph of Aaronson, Jones, and Rutherford upon which he had been basing much of his evidence that the Party was deliberately changing history. Even without the physical photograph, the image still exists in Winston's memory, and O'Brien uses this image as an example of Winston's inability to want to change for the better—the better of the Party.

O'Brien tells Winston that Julia has betrayed him, but there is no evidence in this chapter to prove that it is true. Winston has not betrayed Julia, and that fact is the only thing that keeps him from being "reintegrated"—the only thing keeping him human.

Chapters IV and V

Summary

Winston is still in the Ministry of Truth, but the torture has lessened, and his physical condition is improving. He dreams of sitting in the Golden Country with his mother, Julia, and O'Brien, talking of peaceful things.

He discovers that the Party had been watching him very closely for seven years and that they even have soundtracks and photographs of him and Julia. He realizes the futility of his decision to set himself up against the Party.

During one of his dreams, he wakes up shouting Julia's name and realizes that he will have to start the reintegration process all over. After a moment, O'Brien comes in and orders him to Room 101, the mysterious place where the third stage of Winston's reintegration takes place.

Once in Room 101, Winston faces his greatest fear. O'Brien shows Winston a cage-like mask filled with hungry rats and clicks a door inside it open. One more click and the rats will feast on Winston's face. O'Brien begins to settle the mask over Winston's head when Winston shouts, "Do it to Julia! Do it to Julia! Not me! . . .." O'Brien clicks the cage door shut.

Commentary

Winston again dreams of the Golden Country, his nostalgic place where everything is peaceful. Ironically, he dreams of O'Brien being there; his torturer has become his only friend, an example of *doublethink*, being able to hold two opposing ideas at the same time and believe absolutely in them both.

Like every person, Winston has a breaking point, and O'Brien has found it: rats. The seemingly unimportant scene earlier in the story where Winston becomes terrified of the rats in Mr. Charrington's upstairs room betrayed his phobia. The Party indeed knows everything about its constituents, including how to get inside their minds—something that Julia and Winston did not believe possible.

The fact that Winston betrays Julia is the ultimate irony; the Party has succeeded in making the couple stop loving each other, effectively destroying the only thing that they believed made them human. Remaining human was Winston's only goal, to keep the few centimeters within his head his own; however, the Party does own everything and only for the sake of owning it.

Winston betrays Julia to save himself, a human act of self-preservation, even though the self is supposed to be reserved for the use of the Party. By saving himself, Winston commits a selfish act, and thus should be punished for it; however, he is spared. This can be seen as a flaw in the story.

Glossary

premonitory advising or warning in advance; foreboding.

Chapter VI

Summary

Winston is at the Chestnut Tree Cafe, drinking Victory Gin and listening to the telescreens. At an announcement about the war with the Eurasian army, Winston feels a mixture of excitement and dread. He seems concerned about the outcome of today's battles. He writes in the dust on the table: 2 + 2 = 5.

Winston remembers a time in the recent past in which he saw Julia by accident. She seemed changed, thicker somehow. They both confessed to betraying each other. Winston did not feel that he was in danger in speaking with her; quite the contrary. Winston's life has changed; he no longer works at his former job, and no one seems to care much what he does. He has a vivid memory of his mother and sister and pushes it out of his mind, positive that it is false.

The telescreen announces victory at the front lines, and Winston is overjoyed to tears. In the end, he is happy to have won the struggle over himself; he loves Big Brother.

Commentary

Totalitarianism has won over humanity; Winston is one of the masses now, putting his real self aside for the Party, for Big Brother. Still, he has ambiguous feelings and is haunted by memories of a former time, but he has effectively convinced himself that these feelings and memories are false.

The meeting with Julia resolves some unanswered questions: She did indeed betray Winston, in the same way that he betrayed her. She is becoming like the other women in the novel, sexless and undesirable, just as a woman of the Inner Party should be. When Winston and Julia meet, they repeat each other's phrases, just like Mr. Charrington did earlier in the story, a subtle device to show that they are truly indoctrinated. They are using the diction and the speech patterns of the Party.

Ultimately, Winston loves Big Brother, and will, presumably, spend the rest of his life loving him and waiting for the bullet in the back of his neck to set him free.

Appendix

Summary

The appendix to *1984* is Orwell's explanation of Oceania's official language, Newspeak, of which there are many examples throughout the text, such as *doublethink* and *duckspeak*, and discusses the purpose for its conception.

Newspeak consists of the A vocabulary, the B vocabulary, and the C vocabulary. The A vocabulary consists of words needed for everyday life and words that already exist but have been stripped of all shades of meaning.

The B vocabulary consists of words that have been deliberately constructed for political purposes and are a kind of verbal shorthand; all are compound words, such as *goodthink*.

The C vocabulary consists entirely of scientific and technical words and follows the same grammatical rules as the A and B vocabularies.

Commentary

Newspeak was designed to diminish thought rather than help expression, as is the goal of other languages. Again unlike other languages, Newspeak regularly loses words instead of gains them.

Newspeak is a brilliant device on Orwell's part and serves his political agenda well: If a government can control language, it can also control thought. If there is no word for the concept of *freedom*, how can a person think about *freedom*? By limiting language, the people who speak that language are limited to what concepts exist in words.

Theme

Orwell was convinced that language deteriorated under totalitarian rule and that literature was impossible under totalitarian circumstances. As a writer, Orwell was concerned with the state of language in the world and wrote essays on the effect of governments on writers and writing. Newspeak stems naturally out of Orwell's ideas about language and governmental control.

Orwell predicted that Newspeak would be perfected in the year 2050, perhaps because he wanted to keep the fear of totalitarianism alive in his readers past the year 1984. Orwell was a visionary, predicting many things that eventually came to pass. Thankfully Newspeak is not one of them.

CHARACTER ANALYSES

The following critical analyses delve into the physical, emotional, and psychological traits of the literary work's major characters so that you might better understand what motivates these characters. The writer of this study guide provides this scholarship as an educational tool by which you may compare your own interpretations of the characters. Before reading the character analyses that follow, consider first writing your own short essays on the characters as an exercise by which you can test your understanding of the original literary work. Then, compare your essays to those that follow, noting discrepancies between the two. If your essays appear lacking, that might indicate that you need to re-read the original literary work or re-familiarize yourself with the major characters.

Winston Smith

Winston Smith is the protagonist of *1984*. He is the character that the reader most identifies with, and the reader sees the world from his point of view. Winston is a kind of innocent in a world gone wrong, and it is through him that the reader is able to understand and feel the suffering that exists in the totalitarian society of Oceania.

Even Winston's name is suggestive. *Winston* is taken from Winston Churchill, the exalted leader of wartime England, and *Smith* is the most common last name in the English language, thus allowing readers to see him as Orwell intended: an ordinary man who makes a valiant effort in extraordinary circumstances. A reader cannot resist identifying with Winston: He is ordinary, yet he finds the strength to try and make his circumstances better. He represents the feelings in every human being, and it is for this reason that a reader hopes that things will change. Orwell characterizes Winston as a complete, sympathetic human being, and in doing so gives the reader a stake in the outcome of the novel.

Because Winston is so real, so common, it is easy for readers to identify with him and to imagine themselves in his place. Perhaps Winston carries even more weight for today's reader, who can imagine the possibility of a society like Winston's, the value of technology over humanity.

Even though Winston's life is replete with misery and pain, Orwell allows him a brief time of happiness and love. During this time, there is hope for Winston, and subsequently, hope for the future. But Orwell makes certain that there is no happy ending. Totalitarianism does not permit such an ending; Winston must be crushed. If Winston were to escape, Orwell's agenda of showing the true nature of totalitarianism would have been lost.

Readers identify so closely with Winston because he has individuality and undying self-determination. Winston embodies the values of a civilized society: democracy, peace, freedom, love, and decency. When Winston is destroyed, these things are destroyed with him, and so goes the reader's faith that these values are undying and a natural part of being human. Winston represents the struggle between good and bad forces, and there is no mistaking where the lines are drawn.

Ultimately, Winston loses his spirit and his humanity, the two characteristics that he fought so hard to keep. Orwell insists that Winston's fate could happen to anyone, and it is for this reason that Orwell destroys Winston in the end, so that the reader may understand Orwell's warning and see that the society of *1984* never come to pass.

Julia

Julia is Winston's love-interest and his ally in the struggle against Big Brother. She represents the elements of humanity that Winston does not: pure sexuality, cunning, and survival. While Winston simply manages to survive, Julia is a true survivalist, using any means necessary to conduct her self-centered rebellion. Her demeanor is that of a zealous Party follower, but just under that thin surface is an individual with unchecked human desires and a willful spirit, which ultimately results in her capture.

While Winston enjoys sex and intimacy, Julia is an outwardly sexual being and sleeps with Party members regularly—at least before she meets Winston. She does not do this to destroy the Party but to quench her own desires, and that is the fundamental difference between Winston and Julia. His rebellion is as much for future generations as it is for himself; her rebellion is purely incidental to her own desires.

Julia is far more intuitive and realistic than Winston. She understands the Party better than he does and is more cunning in the ways that she defies Party doctrine. While Winston is emotional about the Party and its potential downfall, Julia feels his wishes are merely fantasy and is apathetic to the Party's dogma. She busies herself with getting around the Party, unlike Winston, who wishes to attack the Party at its center.

Julia uses sex to attack the Party, but it is far less effective a weapon than love. When Julia and Winston fall in love, they commit the ultimate offense against the Party. Note that the couple was caught at their happiest moment, the moment where they let down their guard and felt like an ordinary couple. Both had been watched for years and could have been captured at any time. But not until their love was strong did the Party intervene. Separating the couple diminishes their effectiveness: As individuals they do not understand the party wholly, nor are they capable of resistance.

Superficially, Julia seems like an uncomplicated character. She functions as a sounding board for Winston, but she is far more complicated than that. Winston has real antipathy toward women resulting from the Party's indoctrination and from its stringent sexual codes. Winston can remember a time when affection was shown for affection's sake and is angry at women for what the Party has done to them. Julia does not follow these strict sexual codes and, in fact, breaks them at every opportunity. She shows Winston, who once imagined raping and killing her, that the Party cannot get to the most intimate places in a human being's mind; she is his proof that the feelings that he has been having are valid. Julia gives Winston hope, and it is the continuation of this hope that gets them both destroyed.

O'Brien

O'Brien is a prominent leader in the Inner Party, although his official title is not clear. He seems to be close to Big Brother and may even be part of a collective that makes up Big Brother. O'Brien seems to be a co-conspirator and friend to Winston until the third part of the novel, when he is revealed as a zealous Party leader who had been closely watching Winston for years.

O'Brien represents the Party and all of its contradictions and cruelty. He functions largely to bring the reader into the inner chambers of the Party so that its mechanisms can be revealed. Without O'Brien, the Party would be as mysterious to the reader as it is to Winston and Julia.

While Winston is characterized as an individual, a small man in a large society, O'Brien is bigger than life and remains so throughout the novel. This effect is partly a result of his mysteriousness and partly because the novel hinges on O'Brien's "turnabout" actions; if he were given more time on the page, his true nature would have been revealed too soon.

O'Brien is not only duplicitous in nature, but he also seems to be able to employ *doublethink* very well. Whether or not he truly believes contradictory notions simultaneously, he is determined to teach Winston to do so. There is no evidence to sustain the idea that O'Brien truly believes in the concepts that he forces upon Winston beyond his statement to Winston in the Ministry of Love that the Party had gotten him (O'Brien) long ago.

This statement illustrates a consciousness that would be dangerous for an Outer Party member to have, so it is possible that O'Brien shares the same consciousness as Winston, but because of his status in the Party, has no reason to want society to change. He is not the individual being tortured, though he would have Winston and the reader believe that the "rehabilitation" once happened to him as well.

O'Brien is often seen as a father figure and a friend to Winston. O'Brien is trying, through torture, to make Winston "perfect," to "save" him. If Winston would simply embrace the Party's doctrine, he would be "clean." But it is not really Winston that O'Brien and the Party want to change; the Party wants to purify all thought, believing that one stray thought has the potential to corrupt the Party.

The character of O'Brien is not so different from many of the contemporary leaders of the 20th century. For example, Hitler and Stalin used this kind of torture to keep their power and did it in the name of "purity." O'Brien represents these leaders and others, who use cruelty and torture as their primary method of control.

Big Brother/Emmanuel Goldstein

Big Brother and Emmanuel Goldstein are the conceptual leaders of the opposing forces in Oceania: Big Brother is the titular head of Oceania, and Goldstein is the leader of his opponents, the Brotherhood. They are similar in that Orwell does not make clear whether they actually exist.

Using doublethink, O'Brien tells Winston that Big Brother does and does not exist. Big Brother does exist as the embodiment of the Party, but he can never die. O'Brien will not tell Winston whether Goldstein and the Brotherhood exists, but it is likely that both are merely Party propaganda; the fact that O'Brien claims to have written Goldstein's book is a good indication of this.

Big Brother is aptly named for his position in Oceania—a name of trust, protection, and affection—another example of *doublethink*. Big Brother, or, the Party, is as unlike a benevolent big brother as Hitler or Stalin. Orwell gave Emmanuel Goldstein a traditionally Jewish name that is suggestive of the power structure in World War II. Noteworthy is that *Emmanuel* literally means "God."

It makes no difference in Winston's life whether these two forces exist. Winston's fate is sealed, as is the fate of the society in which he lives, regardless of their existence. Big Brother and Goldstein exist in effect, and that is the only thing that matters to Winston. Orwell intended for these figures to represent totalitarian power structures; in essence, they are both the same. O'Brien, in his incarnation as a Brotherhood leader, asks Winston and Julia if they are willing to commit atrocities against the Party, many of which are no better that the atrocities that the Party commits against its people. Political extremism, as Orwell shows, is not positive under any name.

CRITICAL ESSAYS

On the pages that follow, the writer of this study guide provides critical scholarship on various aspects of George Orwell's *1984*. These interpretive essays are intended solely to enhance your understanding of the original literary work; they are supplemental materials and are not to replace your reading of *1984*. When you're finished reading *1984*, and prior to your reading this study guide's critical essays, consider making a bulleted list of what you think are the most important themes and symbols. Write a short paragraph under each bullet explaining *why* you think that theme or symbol is important; include at least one short quote from the original literary work that supports your contention. Then, test your list and reasons against those found in the following essays. Do you include themes and symbols that the study guide author doesn't? If so, this self test might indicate that you are well on your way to understanding original literary work. But if not, perhaps you will need to re-read *1984*.

The Role of Language and the Act of Writing in Orwell's *1984*

Newspeak, the "official" language of Oceania, functions as a devise of extreme Party control: If the Party is able to control thought, it can also control action. In the year 1984, Newspeak is not fully employed, and for good reason; we would not understand the novel otherwise. However, Orwell makes certain to choose a date, 2050, when Newspeak will be the only language anyone will understand. Even though the year 1984 has passed, the book is still timely due to Orwell's vision and foresight. The decline of language troubled Orwell, who was a writer with political and historical agendas. If language could change for the worse, then truth could change into lies, and that was something that Orwell fought against, both in his personal life and in his writing.

The Purpose of Newspeak

Orwell was sure that the decline of a language had political and economic causes. Although he had no solid proof, he presumed that the languages of countries under dictatorships, such as the Soviet Union or Germany, had deteriorated under their respective regimes. "When the general atmosphere is bad, language must suffer," Orwell writes in his essay, "Politics and the English Language." "If thought corrupts language, language can also corrupt thought," he continues. Here is the very concept behind the invention of Newspeak.

To illustrate this idea that language can corrupt thought and that totalitarian systems use language to restrict, rather than broaden, ideas, Orwell created Newspeak, the official language of Oceania. Without a word for freedom, for example, the concept of freedom cannot exist.

In his Appendix, Orwell explains the syntactical arrangement and the etymology of the Newspeak. A living language, such as English, one that has the capability of diverse expression, has the tendency to *gain* words and therefore broaden the awareness and knowledge of its speakers. Newspeak, on the other hand, *loses* words, by removing words that represent opposing concepts. Therefore, for example, because the word "good" presumes the opposite of "bad," the word "bad" is unnecessary. Similarly, all degrees of "goodness" can be expressed simply by adding standard prefixes and suffixes to this one root word: ungood (bad) and plusgood (very good) and doubleplusgood (wonderful). In so doing, Newspeak not only eliminates "unnecessary" words, but it also promotes a narrowing of thought and, therefore, awareness. The idea behind Newspeak is that, as language must become *less* expressive, the mind is more easily controlled. Through his creation and explanation of Newspeak, Orwell warns the reader that a government that creates the language and mandates how it is used can control the minds of its citizens.

The Role of the Author

George Orwell lived in a time in which he felt oppressed in terms of his writing—publication was difficult in general, and his important work, *Animal Farm,* for example, had a difficult time finding a publisher. So it is not hard to see why he made Winston a kind of writer, giving him such an intense urge to write that Winston risks his existence to begin a journal. Winston's work in the Records Department is also a kind of writing, even though he is essentially producing propaganda that he knows to be lies. Orwell plainly reveals some of his own frustrations about the challenges of being a writer in a highly political time, war time and post-war Europe, through Winston's experience.

Orwell uses writing and the role of the author to illustrate the particular horror of the environment in *1984.* The printed word in *1984* is so dangerous, most books are banned. Winston even has to toss away Julia's note professing her love for fear that three words printed on a scrap of paper would have them both "vaporized." Letters to others are checked off according to purpose, books are written by machines, and many of the acceptable canonized writers, such as Shakespeare, are translated (mutilated) into Newspeak. In Orwell's Oceania, in fact, authors are essentially "vaporized." With books written by machine, the artist is useless. Orwell further emphasizes the danger to literature by having Shakespeare "translated" into Newspeak, effectively destroying that as well.

Orwell also uses the book supposedly written by Emmanuel Goldstein, enemy of the people, as a "bible" of sorts to show how the pen is indeed mightier than the sword, at least in theory. Of course, whether the book—and even its claimed author, Goldstein—is an authentic revolutionary document itself or an elaborate lie of the Party is purposefully left unclear. In *1984,* Orwell strongly implies that even this book is a forgery.

The Mutability of History in *1984*

One of the issues raised in *1984* is the idea that history is mutable or changeable, that truth is what the Party deems it to be, and that the truths found in history are the bases of the principles of the future. Some Fascist German leaders of the time boasted that if you tell a lie loud enough and often enough, people will accept it as truth. The Stalinists perfected this modus operandi by re-writing people and events in and out of history or distorting historical facts to suit the Party's purposes. "Who controls the past controls the future: who controls the present controls the past," runs the Party slogan in *1984*.

Winston's position in the Ministry of Truth is that of creating or forging the past into something unrecognizable to any person with an accurate memory (even memory is controlled in *1984*) so that each forgery "becomes" historic fact. One moment, Oceania is and always has been at war with one enemy, the next moment it is and has always been at war with another, and the people of Oceania accept the information as true. It is an exaggeration of a phenomenon that Orwell observed in his own time and reported with true clarity in *1984*: People most readily believe that which they can believe most conveniently.

The novel makes the distinction between *truth* (the *actual* issues and circumstances of an event) and *fact* (what are *believed* to be the issues and circumstances of an event) and then explores the social-polit-ical-ethical-moral nuances of the evil manipulation of facts in order to control individuals and societies for political gain. Orwell was concerned that the concept of truth was fading out of the world. After all, in the arena of human intercourse of which politics is a part, what is believed is much more powerful than what is actual. If the leaders of nations are the people dictating the what, where, when, who, and how of history, there can be little question that lies find their way into the history books, that those lies are taught to school children, and that they eventually become historical fact.

This concern is quite obvious in *1984*. During Orwell's time as a resistance fighter in Spain, he experienced this rewriting of history first-hand: He noticed that newspaper stories were often inaccurate: There were often reports of battles where no fighting had occurred or no report at all of battles where hundreds of men had died. Orwell conceded that much of history was lies, and he was frustrated by the fact that he believed that history *could* be accurately written.

This "rewriting" of events is not reserved for totalitarian governments. Even in our own time, candidates for all levels of government, including those for President, "remember" things differently, and politicos nationwide attempt to put their "spin" on events that affect us all. It is as if an event can be stricken from history if the population does not remember it. And again, at all levels, non-specific or ambiguous language is used to shade or change the actual events to favor the candidates' or leaders' position or ideology. With every era, our "heroes" are disclaimed, and history books rewritten. As the culture and the ideology change, history changes. Sometimes these distortions are innocent and innocuous differences of perspective; other times, they are deadly dangerous.

CliffsNotes Review

Use this CliffsNotes Review to test your understanding of the original text and reinforce what you've learned in this book. After you work through the review and essay questions, identify the quote section, and the fun and useful practice projects, you're well on your way to understanding a comprehensive and meaningful interpretation of *1984*.

Q&A

1. The Party slogans—War Is Peace, Freedom Is Slavery, Ignorance Is Strength—are examples of

   a. Old Speak
   b. Newspeak
   c. Doublethink

2. What does the paperweight breaking symbolize?

   a. totalitarianism
   b. the shattering of Winston's and Julia's relationship
   c. Big Brother

3. Winston's initial assumption about "the place where there is no darkness" and what it actually turns out to be is an example of

   a. irony
   b. doublethink
   c. ambiguity

4. In what year will Newspeak be fully functional?

   a. 1986
   b. 2002
   c. 2050

5. What does the image of the future look like, according to O'Brien?

   a. a shattered paperweight
   b. a grey, bombed out building
   c. a boot stamping on a human face

   Answers: (1) c. (2) b. (3) a. (4) c. (5) c.

Identify the Quote: Find Each Quote in *1984*

1. Momentarily he caught O'Brien's eye. O'Brien had stood up. He had take off his spectacles and was in the act of resettling them on his nose with his characteristic gesture. But there was a fraction of a second when their eyes met, and for long as it took to happen Winston knew—yes, he *knew*—that O'Brien was thinking the same thing as himself.

2. Freedom is the freedom to say that two plus two make four. If that is granted, all else follows.

3. I don't mean confessing. Confession is not betrayal. What you say or do doesn't matter; only feelings matter. If they could make me stop loving you—that would be the real betrayal.

4. You are prepared, the two of you, to separate and never see one another again?

5. We are the dead.

6. If you want a picture of the future, imagine a boot stamping on a human face—forever.

7. You are the last man. You are the guardian of the human spirit. You shall see yourself as you are. Take off your clothes.

8. Do it to Julia! Do it to Julia! Not me! Julia! I don't care what you do to her. Tear her face off, strip her to the bones. Not me! Julia! Not me!

Answers: (1) [The omniscient narrator to the reader, explaining the moment in the Two Minute's Hate when Winston is mistakenly certain that O'Brien is a co-conspirator.] (2) [Winston writing in his diary; this is the quote that becomes the sticking point between Winston and O'Brien.] (3) [Winston to Julia, discussing what they will do when they are caught and arrested.] (4) [O'Brien to Winston and Julia, when he is inculturating them into the Brotherhood.] (5) [Winston to Julia, the moment before they are captured.] (6) [O'Brien to Winston during a torture session.] (7) [O'Brien to Winston. After many months of torture, O'Brien shows Winston his ruined body in the mirror.] (8) [Winston to O'Brien—the ultimate betrayal in Room 101, when he loses what is left of his humanity.]

Essay Questions

1. Although O'Brien confirms the existence of Big Brother, he refuses to to confirm or deny the existence of the Brotherhood. Discuss the role of the Brotherhood in the dynamics of Oceania's society and in the novel.

2. Orwell wrote *1984* as a warning. Explain what he was warning people about. Be sure to examine the influence of political climates in the world during the time when Orwell wrote.

3. Explain in what ways Julia differs from Winston. Consider her behavior, her motivation, and her goals.

4. *1984* is rife with irony (that is, things being different from what is expected) and doublethink (being able to absolutely believe in two opposing ideas simultaneously). Divide a piece of paper into two columns. On one side, list as many examples of doublthink as you can can; on the other, list examples of irony. Discuss what you think Orwell's purpose was in using both.

Practice Projects

1. Create a report on the similarities between Orwell's Oceania and some current or past totalitarian regime. In doing so, consider the role of children and family, the idea of "thoughtcrimes," the re-creation of history, and the use of propoaganda.

2. Draw a map of the political structure of the world of *1984*. Write a diary entry imagining that you are in Winston's world and describe how you feel and what you do on a daily basis, and detail your future plans. How is this entry different from one you might write in your present position?

3. Create a Web site to introduce *1984* to other readers. Design pages to intrigue and inform your audience, and invite other readers to post their thoughts and responses to their reading of the novel.

4. Referring to the Appendix to the novel, rewrite the Second Amendment of the United States Constitution (or some other text) to conform to the standards of Newspeak. Discuss what meaning, if any, is lost in the translation.

CliffsNotes Resource Center

The learning doesn't need to stop here. CliffsNotes Resource Center shows you the best of the best—links to the best information in print and online about the author and/or related works. And don't think that this is all we've prepared for you; we've put all kinds of pertinent information at www.cliffsnotes.com. Look for all the terrific resources at your favorite bookstore or local library and on the Internet. When you're online, make your first stop www.cliffsnotes.com where you'll find more incredibly useful information about *1984*.

Books

This CliffsNotes book, published by Wiley Publishing, Inc. provides a meaningful interpretation of *1984*. If you are looking for information about the author and/or related works, check out these other publications:

The Language of **1984**: *Orwell's Language and Ours,* by W. F. Bolton. A study of Orwell's attitudes toward and use of English realating to how the language has developed since his death. Oxford and London: Basil Balckwell and Andre Deutsch, 1984.

George Orwell: A Life, by Bernard Crick. The preeminent Orwell biographer delves into Orwell's life and work. London: Seker and Warburg, 1980. Reprint. Harmondsworth, England, Penguin Books, 1982.

A George Orwell Companion, by J. R. Hammond, offers biographical information, as well as studies of Orwell's work. New York: St. Martin's Press, 1982.

The Future of **Nineteen Eighty-Four,** edited by Ejner J. Jensen, includes essays about *1984*. Ann Arbor: University of Michigan Press, 1984.

Homage to Oceania: The Prophetic Vision of George Orwell, by Ruth Ann Leif, discusses Orwell's political agendas and ideals. Columbus: Ohio State University Press, 1969.

On **Nineteen Eighty-Four.** Peter Stansky, ed. Essays on Orwell and *1984* by scholars at Stanford University. New York and San Francisco: W.H. Freeman & Co., 1983.

***George Orwell and the Origins of* 1984,** by William Steinhoff, offers a comprehensive study of *1984*. Ann Arbor: University of Michigan Press, 1975.

It's easy to find books published by Wiley Publishing, Inc. You'll find them in your favorite bookstores (on the Internet and at a store near you). We also have three web sites that you can use to read about all the books we publish:

- `www.cliffsnotes.com`

- `www.dummies.com`

- `www.wiley.com`

Internet

Check out these Web resources for more information about George Orwell and *1984*:

The Chestnut Tree Café, `http://www.seas.upenn.edu/~allport/chestnut/chestnut.htm`—This site is a Web page devoted to exploring the life, times, and work of Orwell. It includes his essays, critical essays, and a biography.

George Orwell, `http://www.codoh.com/thoughtcrimes/tcportorw.html`—A short biography and a link to the "Thoughtcrimes Archive," a list of people recently persecuted for being freethinkers.

George Orwell, `http://www.uv.es/~fores/orwell.html`— A biography and links to other Orwell sites.

The Internet Movie Database, `http://us.imdb.com/M/person-exact?+Orwell,+George`—Extensive filmography of all of Orwell's works.

George Orwell 1903–1950, `http://www.k-1.com/Orwell/1984.htm`—Offers summary, plot, characters, and interpretation of *1984*.

Charles' George Orwell Links, http://pages.citenet.net/
users/charles/links.html—Some great links as well as the
entire novel on the Web.

Next time you're on the Internet, don't forget to drop by
www.cliffsnotes.com. We created an online Resource Center that
you can use today, tomorrow, and beyond.

Other Works by Orwell

While reading all of Orwell's work will help a reader to better
understand the novel *1984*, the following Orwell titles may be the most
helpful:

Animal Farm, by George Orwell. Another novel about the effects of totalitarianism on the human spirit, as told allegorically through a group
of barnyard animals. New York, Harcourt, Brace & Company,
1946.

Homage to Catalonia, by George Orwell. Orwell's memoir of his time
in Franco's Spain. Politics features prominently. London: Secker &
Warburg, 1938. Boston: Beacon Press, 1952.

Shooting an Elephant and Other Essays, by George Orwell. Orwell's
posthumously published essays. Readers will learn a good deal about
Orwell's political ideas from this collection. London: Seker & Warburg, 1950.

Send Us Your Favorite Tips

In your quest for knowledge, have you ever experienced that sub-
lime moment when you figure out a trick that saves time or trouble?
Perhaps you realized you were taking ten steps to accomplish something that could have taken two. Or you found a little-known
workaround that achieved great results. If you've discovered a useful
tip that gave you insight into or helped you understand 1984 and you'd
like to share it, the CliffsNotes staff would love to hear from you. Go
to our Web site at www.cliffsnotes.com and click the Talk to Us
button. If we select your tip, we may publish it as part of CliffsNotes
Daily, our exciting, free e-mail newsletter. To find out more or to sub-
scribe to a newsletter, go to www.cliffsnotes.com on the Web.

Index

NUMBERS

CliffsNotes

LITERATURE NOTES

CliffsNotes Guides

TECHNOLOGY TOPICS

PERSONAL FINANCE TOPICS

CAREER TOPICS